THIS PLANNER BELONGS TO:

_____

ONE Question A DAY

WEEKLY PLANNER

365 PROMPTS FOR A MEANINGFUL YEAR

CASTLE POINT BOOKS

ONE QUESTION A DAY WEEKLY PLANNER.
Copyright © 2024 by St. Martin's Press.
All rights reserved. Printed in Turkey.
For information, address St. Martin's Publishing Group,
120 Broadway, New York, NY 10271.

www.castlepointbooks.com

The Castle Point Books trademark is owned by Castle Point Publishing, LLC.
Castle Point books are published and distributed by St. Martin's Publishing Group.

ISBN 978-1-250-35877-6 (flexibound)

Our books may be purchased in bulk for promotional, educational,
or business use. Please contact your local bookseller or the Macmillan
Corporate and Premium Sales Department at 1-800-221-7945,
extension 5442, or by email at MacmillanSpecialMarkets@macmillan.com.

First Edition: 2024

10 9 8 7 6 5 4 3 2 1

SELF-DISCOVERY AND JOYFUL PAUSES SHOULD ALWAYS BE PART OF THE PLAN!

The *One Question a Day Weekly Planner* is designed to help you stay on schedule and add a meaningful moment to each day. Whether it's jotting down last night's dream, spilling a juicy secret, or expressing gratitude for small wonders, taking time to reflect is beneficial to your health and happiness. Let this planner be your daily reminder to slow down and savor the glimmers and treasures that make an ordinary day special.

Start with your goals and intentions for the month ahead and move forward with purpose and momentum. Fill in the date at the top of each weekly planner page and pencil in all your scheduled activities. Get in the habit of answering the daily prompt each morning or evening. Don't overthink it. Just record the first response that comes to mind. Later on, you can look back on this time capsule of your year and gain new insights.

With prompts ranging from lighthearted to deep, every page of the *One Question a Day Weekly Planner* helps you reduce anxiety and simply enjoy the moment.

°∘° YOU IN THIS MOMENT °∘°

Capture who you are in this moment by adding your
answers to this page. Come back later to see how your
answers have (or haven't) changed over time.

Describe yourself in three words.

List three people, activities, or places that bring you the most joy.

Name one thing you're struggling with.

Describe this stage of your life.

List any milestones you're approaching.
How do you feel about them?

List three personal goals.

List three career goals.

List three relationship goals.

INTENTIONS FOR THE MONTH OF _____

The best thing about this month:

_____
_____
_____
_____
_____

One wish I hope comes true:

_____
_____
_____
_____

Top goal for the coming weeks:

_____
_____
_____
_____

Something I can do this month that reflects my values:

My self-care mantra:

New places, habits, or things I'd like to try:

WEEK OF _____

M

How can you find peace today?

T

What will go even better today than it did yesterday?

W

Who do you hope you run into today?

T

What did you learn today?

If you could rewind the day, what would you do differently?

What kind words could you offer yourself today?

Rate your mood today from 1 (grrr) to 10 (fist pump).

WEEK OF _____

M	Who could you introduce yourself to today?
T	Which contact texted you the most today?
W	Who is the first person you thought of today?
T	What little white lie did you tell today?

What are you excited or anxious about?

If today were a book, what would the title be?

How relaxed do you feel right now?

WEEK OF _____

M

What are you waiting for?

T

What are you working on?

W

What would be the perfect way to end this day?

T

What had you laughing out loud?

How did fortune favor you today?

What has always been true for you?

What did you accomplish today, and how can you celebrate?

F

S

S

NOTES

WEEK OF _____

M	What plans could you make to shake up the week?
T	What would add a dose of joy to this day?
W	What might help you sleep better tonight?
T	What was the most meaningful moment of your day?

What new habit could you start today?

What's your top priority for today?

What have you been meaning to get around to?

F

S

S

NOTES

WEEK OF _____

M

What gives you a sense of purpose?

T

How could you get some fresh air today?

W

What did you think when you looked in the mirror today?

T

What were you too hard on yourself about today?

What makes you excited about the future?

What could you get rid of today?

What brilliant idea could you make happen?

F

S

S

NOTES

INTENTIONS FOR THE MONTH OF _____

The best thing about this month:

_____

_____

_____

_____

One wish I hope comes true:

_____

_____

_____

_____

Top goal for the coming weeks:

_____

_____

_____

_____

Something I can do this month that reflects my values:

_____

_____

_____

_____

My self-care mantra:

_____

_____

_____

_____

New places, habits, or things I'd like to try:

_____

_____

_____

_____

WEEK OF _____

M

What could you slow down and enjoy today?

T

When do you know you need a break from social media?

W

What did you take pride in today?

T

Do a little self-check. How are you feeling?

What makes today new and different?

How much time did you reserve for yourself today?

What was the best choice you made today?

WEEK OF _____

M	What vibes are you sending out today?
T	What is your inner voice saying?
W	What alter ego could help you conquer the day?
T	Who has your back today?

What did you need a friend for today?

When have you caused a little mischief?

What color best describes you today? Why?

WEEK OF _____

M

Where do you want to go today?

T

How did you go with the flow today?

W

Who could you surprise today?

T

Choose three words to describe yourself.

What's one thing you'd never do?

What club, class, or adventure could you sign up for today?

Describe what happy feels like to you.

WEEK OF _____

M	Where could you find peace today?
T	What lesson have you learned recently?
W	Who or what are you the boss of?
T	What is your best-kept secret?

If the power went out, what would you do to keep busy?

What does it feel good to know?

This is the perfect day to _____.

WEEK OF _____

M

How much alone time do you need each day?

T

How might today be a fresh start?

W

Who do you love with all your heart?

T

What area of your life needs attention right now?

What was the pinnacle of your day?

What are you grateful for today?

What do you love most about how you look today?

F

S

S

NOTES

The best thing about this month:

One wish I hope comes true:

Top goal for the coming weeks:

Something I can do this month that reflects my values:

My self-care mantra:

New places, habits, or things I'd like to try:

WEEK OF _____

M

Who is good for a laugh today?

T

What are you afraid to admit to yourself or others?

W

What news did you hear today?

T

How can you make the best of today's weather?

What was the easiest part of your day so far?

What was the hardest part of your day so far?

How are you winning at life?

WEEK OF _____

M

What could you take less seriously?

T

What could you take more seriously?

W

Who made you feel seen today?

T

What are you excited to be a part of?

What surprised you today?

How would you rate the kindness of strangers today?

What connection did you make today?

WEEK OF _____

M

What could you interpret as a sign today?

T

When did you let your voice be heard?

W

How could you add a little romance to the day?

T

What sounds are a comfort to you?

How far have you come?

What would you tell your younger self?

Write a short note to your future self.

WEEK OF _____

M

Look around. What do you notice?

T

List your top three moments from this day.

W

How could you get cozy today?

T

How do you jumpstart a boring day?

List one of your travel goals.

What made today different from every other day?

Write a positive mantra for encouragement today.

WEEK OF _____

M	Picture your favorite place and describe it here.
T	Find a cloud and describe what you see in it.
W	How independent are you?
T	What did you get lost in today?

What show feels like it's about your life?

What is the way to your heart?

What are you struggling with today?

INTENTIONS FOR THE MONTH OF _____

The best thing about this month:

_____
_____
_____
_____
_____

One wish I hope comes true:

_____
_____
_____
_____
_____

Top goal for the coming weeks:

_____
_____
_____
_____
_____

Something I can do this month that reflects my values:

_____
_____
_____
_____

My self-care mantra:

_____
_____
_____
_____

New places, habits, or things I'd like to try:

_____
_____
_____
_____

WEEK OF _____

M

What role do you often play?

T

What is your best quality?

W

Who are the people who love you no matter what?

T

Describe the view outside your window.

How would you describe your attitude today?

What would be the cherry on top of this day?

What are you trying to make sense of?

WEEK OF _____

M

What have you learned about yourself?

T

How would you describe your style today?

W

What matters most today?

T

What is worth fighting for?

What amount of money is enough?

What are you saving for?

What does it comfort you to know?

WEEK OF _____

M	What deserves a five-star rating today?
T	What is the best thing someone could say to you today?
W	What could you do differently today?
T	Which friend deserves a shout-out today?

What makes your life full?

What will you remember most about this day?

What do you love most about your life?

F

S

S

NOTES

WEEK OF _____

M

What song would you dedicate to yourself today?

T

Where do you feel tension today? Why?

W

What would it feel good to say no to today?

T

What is causing you the most stress?

What dish could you treat yourself to today?

Do you live mostly in the past, present, or future?

What life hacks have you developed?

WEEK OF _____

M

What gives you strength?

T

What could you do for a little self-care today?

W

Who makes you want to be a better person?

T

What weakness could you turn into a strength?

What gives you a warm, fuzzy feeling?

Who scares you a little?

What could you set into motion today?

INTENTIONS FOR THE MONTH OF _____

The best thing about this month:

_____
_____
_____
_____
_____

One wish I hope comes true:

_____
_____
_____
_____

Top goal for the coming weeks:

_____
_____
_____
_____
_____

Something I can do this month that reflects my values:

_____

_____

_____

_____

My self-care mantra:

_____

_____

_____

_____

New places, habits, or things I'd like to try:

_____

_____

_____

_____

WEEK OF _____

M	What is your dream vacation?
T	How can you spread positivity today?
W	Who are the most optimistic people you know?
T	What warmed your heart today?

What famous quote or saying best fits this day?

Who needs your guidance most?

If your feelings were weather, what would they be?

WEEK OF _____

M	Who always brings the fun?
T	How could you let your imagination flow today?
W	What do you wonder about?
T	What good habits do you have?

What little luxury makes your day ten times better?

Stop to admire something unique. Describe it here.

What is the theme of your life right now?

WEEK OF _____

M

How organized are you?

T

What is the best part about being a grown-up?

W

What was the best part about being a kid?

T

What's one life lesson you've learned?

What are you confused about?

Who or what are you in awe of?

In what do you put your faith?

WEEK OF _____

M

What change could you make to your routine today?

T

What does your inner rebel want to do today?

W

What beautiful thing did you see today?

T

Who drives you crazy?

Make a prediction.

Write down your favorite joke. Be sure to tell it today.

Did you wander, walk, or race through the day?

WEEK OF _____

M

What have you changed your mind about?

T

What is so you?

W

Who do you look forward to seeing?

T

What promise are you willing to make to yourself or others?

What do you need time to process?

Where do you go to reflect?

How will you know when you've made it?

INTENTIONS FOR THE MONTH OF _____

The best thing about this month:

_____
_____
_____
_____

One wish I hope comes true:

_____
_____
_____
_____

Top goal for the coming weeks:

_____
_____
_____
_____

Something I can do this month that reflects my values:

_____

_____

_____

_____

My self-care mantra:

_____

_____

_____

_____

New places, habits, or things I'd like to try:

_____

_____

_____

_____

WEEK OF _____

M

What could you worry less about?

T

Who adds drama to your day?

W

How do you like to spend your evenings?

T

What do you keep to yourself?

What is today's breaking news?

What could you delegate to someone else today?

What was the most peaceful part of your day?

F

S

S

NOTES

WEEK OF _____

M

If you won the lottery, what would you buy first?

T

How could you express yourself today?

W

What is your newest catch phrase?

T

What swear word do you use the most?

What is worth getting up early for?

Jot down a favorite song lyric. How does it speak to you?

What could you go without today?

F

S

S

NOTES

WEEK OF _____

M

What emoji best describes your mood today? Draw or explain it.

T

Which celebrity do you most want to meet?

W

What makes a day a perfect ten?

T

Who do you need to meet for lunch soon?

What big plans are you excited to make?

What increased your heart rate today?

Who inspires you?

WEEK OF _____

M	What problem did you solve today?
T	What new restaurant could you try today?
W	Are you more the product of nature or nurture?
T	What do you deserve a medal for?

How patient were you today?

What scares you right now?

Who challenges you?

WEEK OF _____

M

How kind have you been to yourself today?

T

What do you need most today?

W

How might you simplify your life?

T

Who is your sidekick?

If you changed your name, what would you change it to?

What could you take a ten-minute break to do?

How satisfied are you with your job?

INTENTIONS FOR THE MONTH OF _____

The best thing about this month:

_____

_____

_____

_____

_____

One wish I hope comes true:

_____

_____

_____

_____

Top goal for the coming weeks:

_____

_____

_____

_____

Something I can do this month that reflects my values:

My self-care mantra:

New places, habits, or things I'd like to try:

WEEK OF _____

M

How well do you handle change?

T

What is the key to your happiness?

W

What do you hope happens today?

T

What could you make today?

How did you begin your day?

What motivates you?

Write three compliments for yourself.

WEEK OF _____

M

What group makes you feel most included?

T

What makes you a good friend?

W

What geographic setting makes you happiest?

T

What is the best thing about being your age?

What small step could you take to get closer to a goal?

What have you lost recently, and what have you gained?

What do you wish your family could understand about you?

WEEK OF _____

M

Where do you need healthier boundaries?

T

Who always tells you the truth?

W

What is fresh and new in your life?

T

What are you still getting used to?

What does your heart want today?

What would make this day brighter?

What seeds could you plant for the future today?

WEEK OF _____

M	What keeps you up at night?
T	Who was the last person you called?
W	What do you rely on?
T	You're stranded on an island. Who do you want with you?

Who fights for you?

What could you reserve time for today?

What area could you spruce up today?

WEEK OF _____

M	How could you unplug today?
T	What could you say yes to today?
W	What does your family understand about you?
T	What's never been better?

The road to happiness is paved with _____.

How could you get your nature fix today?

Who looks up to you?

INTENTIONS FOR THE MONTH OF _____

The best thing about this month:

_____
_____
_____
_____
_____

One wish I hope comes true:

_____
_____
_____
_____
_____

Top goal for the coming weeks:

_____
_____
_____
_____
_____

Something I can do this month that reflects my values:

_____

_____

_____

_____

My self-care mantra:

_____

_____

_____

_____

New places, habits, or things I'd like to try:

_____

_____

_____

_____

WEEK OF _____

M

How have you outdone yourself today?

T

What song would you feature on a soundtrack for today?

W

What isn't fair?

T

Who would you beat in a dance off?

What are you laughably bad at?

What are you surprisingly good at?

Who could you send flowers to today?

WEEK OF _____

M

What are you hoping to prove to yourself or others?

T

Rate your work/life balance on a scale from 1 to 10.

W

How confident do you feel today?

T

When was the last time you had a good cry?

What is the most precious object you own?

What are you passionate about right now?

What do you need reassurance about today?

F

S

S

NOTES

WEEK OF _____

M

What is the word of the day?

T

What trend have you been meaning to try?

W

What did you find triggering today?

T

Who do you work well with?

Which part of this day do you wish you could fast forward?

F

Who do you need space from?

S

What makes you feel lucky?

S

NOTES

WEEK OF _____

M	How do you show that you care?
T	What tiny miracle did you witness today?
W	What are you never too old to do?
T	What are your instincts telling you?

Where could you wander off to today?

If you had a time machine, what year would you visit today?

What words do you live by?

WEEK OF _____

M

What feeling came on strong today?

T

How early is too early to get up?

W

What keeps you up past your bedtime?

T

What is your body telling you today?

What do you see in your near future?

What are you wondering about?

What have you been telling yourself today?

F

S

S

NOTES

INTENTIONS FOR THE MONTH OF _____

The best thing about this month:

_____
_____
_____
_____
_____

One wish I hope comes true:

_____
_____
_____
_____

Top goal for the coming weeks:

_____
_____
_____
_____

Something I can do this month that reflects my values:

My self-care mantra:

New places, habits, or things I'd like to try:

WEEK OF _____

M	What keeps coming back to you?
T	What childhood habit have you kept?
W	What do you love about your home?
T	What are you trying to stay focused on today?

What are you longing for?

What was the highlight of your day?

Who would you be excited to see today?

WEEK OF _____

M

What's one thing the past has taught you?

T

What could you do for yourself today?

W

What do you have control over today?

T

Who's on your team? Who's not?

Who have you won over?

What feels too good to be true?

Which relationship requires the most work?

WEEK OF _____

M	What comes naturally to you?
T	If today were a class, what would be it be called?
W	What job would be perfect for you?
T	What job would be your worst nightmare?

Do you believe in destiny?

What feels like it was meant to be?

Describe what love feels like in three words.

F

S

S

NOTES

WEEK OF _____

M

Describe a dream you remember.

T

Every day is an opportunity to _____.

W

Who deserves your thanks?

T

What are you putting off doing today?

What do you fantasize about doing?

What's the best way to meet new people?

What was in the last package you received?

WEEK OF _____

M

What did you discover today?

T

What always puts you in a good mood?

W

What's the latest gossip?

T

What are you tempted to do today?

What is your mission today?

What are you happy to have in your life?

If you were to start your own company, what would it be?

INTENTIONS FOR THE MONTH OF _____

The best thing about this month:

_____
_____
_____
_____
_____

One wish I hope comes true:

_____
_____
_____
_____
_____

Top goal for the coming weeks:

_____
_____
_____
_____
_____

Something I can do this month that reflects my values:

My self-care mantra:

New places, habits, or things I'd like to try:

WEEK OF _____

M

What makes you weird in the best way?

T

Follow the rules today, or break them?

W

What does healthy mean to you?

T

What are you still learning about yourself?

How anxious are you today on a scale from 1 to 10?

What are you craving today?

What's your favorite nightime ritual?

WEEK OF _____

M

What's the best song to sing in the shower?

T

How overwhelmed do you feel today on a scale from 1 to 10?

W

What thoughts help calm you?

T

What new endeavor could you embark on?

What do you need more than ever?

What's gleaming on the horizon?

Who could you talk to for hours?

WEEK OF _____

M

What are you looking forward to this week?

T

What's no longer serving you?

W

What mistakes did you learn from?

T

What could you try today?

What are you the queen or king of?

The world is my _____.

Where is your happy place?

WEEK OF _____

M

What's food for your soul?

T

What was your biggest purchase so far this week?

W

What would be a brave step for you?

T

What do you believe in?

What line will you never cross?

What is one little thing you can appreciate about today?

What makes you feel like a kid again?

WEEK OF _____

M	Who could you forgive?
T	What change do you feel coming?
W	Who is your frenemy?
T	What are you feeling good about?

Are you a lover or a fighter (or a little of both)?

What are you free to do today?

What could you show off today?

INTENTIONS FOR THE MONTH OF _____

The best thing about this month:

_____

_____

_____

_____

_____

One wish I hope comes true:

_____

_____

_____

_____

_____

Top goal for the coming weeks:

_____

_____

_____

_____

_____

Something I can do this month that reflects my values:

_____

_____

_____

_____

My self-care mantra:

_____

_____

_____

_____

New places, habits, or things I'd like to try:

_____

_____

_____

_____

WEEK OF _____

M

Who underestimates you?

T

What sadness are you carrying? Who can you talk to?

W

How could you nurture a new friendship today?

T

How are you a success?

What are you growing fond of?

Who or what never bores you?

What lifts your spirits?

WEEK OF _____

M

Today is a perfect day to _____.

T

How could you make lemonade out of lemons today?

W

When were you at your best today?

T

What quality do you admire in others?

Where were you ten years ago today?

What did you put most of your energy into today?

List three things that make your day better.

WEEK OF _____

M

How hard did you work today on a scale from 1 to 10?

T

What is the best thing that could happen to you today?

W

What could you pencil into your week?

T

Where do you think you'll be five years from today?

Whose opinion matters most to you?

What idea could you share today?

What was the most satisfying moment of your day?

WEEK OF _____

M

What does the universe seem to be telling you today?

T

Who demands a lot from you?

W

What gift did you receive today?

T

When have you refused to settle?

What do you look for in a good partner?

What side(s) of yourself did you show the world today?

What part of your life needs a makeover?

WEEK OF _____

M

What could you ask for from others today?

T

What pattern have you noticed in yourself or others?

W

How powerful do you feel today?

T

What emotions prevailed today?

What do you need to vent about?

What part of your day was most chaotic?

What bold move could you make today?

INTENTIONS FOR THE MONTH OF _____

The best thing about this month:

_____

_____

_____

_____

One wish I hope comes true:

_____

_____

_____

_____

Top goal for the coming weeks:

_____

_____

_____

_____

Something I can do this month that reflects my values:

My self-care mantra:

New places, habits, or things I'd like to try:

WEEK OF _____

M

What could today be the beginning of?

T

What superpower would be most useful today?

W

If you're the hero of your story, who is the villain?

T

What makes you feel optimistic about the future?

What opportunity could you seize upon today?

What feels impossible?

What depletes your social battery?

WEEK OF _____

M

Where is your safe haven?

T

What's the cutest thing you saw today?

W

Who makes you swoon?

T

What was a pleasant surprise this week?

What are you patiently awaiting?

Who or what do you want to hide from today?

Describe your day in three words.

WEEK OF _____

M

When could you pencil in a mindful break?

T

What served you well today?

W

What podcast could you add to your favorites today?

T

What aspects of social media benefit your life?

What aspects of social media do you try to avoid?

What book are you excited about reading next?

How did you entertain yourself or others today?

WEEK OF _____

M	Do you believe in soulmates? Explain.
T	What makes you lovable?
W	What did you struggle with today?
T	What's the best part about being you?

What will you never part from?

What are the little glimmers that made your day brighter?

Who needs you today?

F

S

S

NOTES

WEEK OF _____

M

What's starting to be a bore?

T

What is there still plenty of time to do?

W

What do you want to remember about this week?

T

How sentimental do you feel today?

What would you put on a vision board?

How could you dream even bigger?

What makes a day go from blah to hoorah?

° ° YOU, ONE YEAR LATER ° °

Fill in your responses, then flip back to
YOU IN THIS MOMENT at the beginning of the planner.
Notice how your answers have evolved.

Describe yourself in three words.

_____

_____

_____

List three people, activities, or places that bring you the most joy.

_____

_____

_____

Name one thing you're struggling with.

_____

Describe this stage of your life.

_____

_____

_____

_____

List any milestones you're approaching.
How do you feel about them?

List three personal goals.

List three career goals.

List three relationship goals.

PROGRESS YOU'VE MADE

REALIZATIONS YOU'VE COME TO

YOUR BEST SELF-CARE TOOLS AND PRACTICES

NOTES AND OTHER DOODADS